slow down

50 MINDFUL MOMENTS IN NATURE

WRITTEN BY

RACHEL WILLIAMS

ILLUSTRATED BY

FREYA HARTAS

MAGIC CAT 🐱 PUBLISHING

NEW YORK

What is this life if, full of care,
We have no time to stand and stare?–

No time to stand beneath the boughs,
And stare as long as sheep or cows:

No time to see, when woods we pass,
Where squirrels hide their nuts in grass:

No time to see, in broad daylight,
Streams full of stars, like skies at night:

No time to turn at Beauty's glance,
And watch her feet, how they can dance:

No time to wait till her mouth can
Enrich that smile her eyes began?

A poor life this if, full of care,
We have no time to stand and stare.

–"Leisure" by W.H. Davies

CONTENTS

1 — SLOW DOWN. STOP. LISTEN.

2 — A BEE POLLINATES A FLOWER

4 — DEW COLLECTS ON A LEAF

6 — A BUTTERFLY EMERGES FROM A CHRYSALIS

8 — A DUCK TEACHES HER DUCKLINGS TO SWIM

10 — A SPIDER WEAVES A WEB

12 — THE DAWN CHORUS PERFORMS

14 — A THUNDERSTORM ON A SUMMER'S DAY

16 — A SQUIRREL BURIES AN ACORN IN AUTUMN
AND DIGS IT UP AGAIN IN WINTER

18 — A BAT GOES HUNTING AT NIGHT

20 — A RAINBOW APPEARS

22 — A FOX EATS BERRIES FROM A BUSH

24 — A SNOWFLAKE FALLS

26 — MAMA AND DADA BIRDS FEED THEIR BABIES

28 — A HONEYBEE HIVE GETS TO WORK

30 — THE MOON WAXES . . . AND WANES

32 — AN OCEAN WAVE FORMS, CRESTS, AND BREAKS

34 — A TADPOLE BECOMES A FROG

36 >< BLUEBELLS TRANSFORM A WOODLAND

38 >< A MOLE TOPS UP HIS STORE OF EARTHWORMS

40 >< A SUNFLOWER TRACKS THE SUN

42 >< A GAME OF CAT AND MOUSE

44 >< A SHOOTING STAR LIGHTS UP THE NIGHT SKY

46 >< A SNAKE SHEDS ITS SKIN

48 >< MUSHROOMS GROW IN A FOREST

50 >< A SPECTACULAR SUNSET DESCENDS

52 >< A SNAIL LEAVES A TRAIL

54 >< A TREE'S LEAVES CHANGE COLOR . . . AND FALL

56 >< A SPARROW TAKES A BATH

58 >< A CLOUD FORMS

60 >< A CHICK HATCHES FROM AN EGG

62 >< CHERRY BLOSSOMS FALL TO THE GROUND

64 >< WEAVER ANTS BUILD A NEST

66 >< FIDDLEHEADS UNFURL IN THE SUNSHINE

68 >< A MOSQUITO MAKES A NARROW ESCAPE

70 >< A WOODPECKER GETS TO WORK

72 >< A SEA STAR SHUFFLES ACROSS THE OCEAN FLOOR

74 >< A DRAGONFLY PERFORMS AN AERIAL SHOW

76 >< WATER LILIES OPEN ON A POND

78 >< A BARN OWL WAKES UP

80 >< POPPIES BLOOM IN A FIELD

82 >< A HORSE GALLOPS THROUGH A MEADOW

84 >< MOSS DRINKS IN A WOODLAND RAIN SHOWER

86 >< A LADYBUG TAKES TO THE AIR

88 >< SALMON SWIM UPSTREAM

90 >< A FLOCK OF GEESE TAKES FLIGHT

92 >< A HARE OUTRUNS A HUNGRY FOX

94 >< A KINGFISHER DIVES UNDERWATER TO CATCH A FISH

96 >< A HARVEST MOUSE SEARCHES FOR SUPPER

98 >< AN OYSTER MAKES A PEARL

100 >< A WOLF HOWLS TO HIS PACK

102 >< SLOW DOWN TODAY

106 >< FURTHER READING

107 >< SELECTED BIBLIOGRAPHY

108 >< INDEX

SLOW DOWN. STOP. LISTEN.

In the early morning light, a bird outside is calling, "Good morning!" He joins in the dawn chorus, which sings their song all year. In a tree next door, the melody sends a little owl to sleep–a gentle lullaby after his long night hunt. And as the owl drifts off, a ladybug drinks the last of the morning dew . . .

All around us, nature is turning, growing . . . and working wonders. Every day, hour by hour, magical transformations happen right in front of our eyes. But it's not always easy to see them.

This book is filled with nature's ordinary events. Told like a story, some of these events happen slowly, over days or weeks–like a butterfly emerging from a chrysalis or a squirrel burying acorns for the winter. Other things happen in a moment–like a sunrise or a cloud forming.

Enjoy each of them, paused just long enough to watch them unfold. And then go outside, to see what you find when you take the time to slow down.

A BEE
POLLINATES A FLOWER

It could be said that a bee's most important job is to pollinate flowers.

Without pollination, plants can't reproduce and fruit can't grow! When a bee collects nectar from a flowering plant, some pollen from the stamen—the male part of the flower—sticks to the hairs on its body.

When the bee visits the next flower, this pollen is rubbed off onto the stigma—the female part of the flower. At this moment, pollination occurs. Watch this happen in a bright, springtime garden . . .

The bee uses her antennae to find the garden's sweetest flowers.

Different types of bees are attracted to different types of flowers.

Peering into the shallow nectar of the flower, the bee dips her tongue in and drinks deeply.

As she drinks, she brushes against the stamens of the flower and pollen sticks to her legs.

She flies to another flower. As she lands and tucks into the nectar, the pollen rubs off her legs onto the flower's stigma.

The flower is now pollinated!

Ready to explore the rest of the garden, the bee looks up to scout her next meal.

And she's off, in search of another flower . . .

DEW COLLECTS ON A LEAF

Nothing welcomes a new day like dew collecting on a leaf.

In the cool morning air, leaves and other plants with flat surfaces collect tiny droplets of water.

You might think the cause could be an overnight rain shower—but it's actually because of something called condensation.

Before dawn, the leaf has cooled down in the cold air. Moisture in the air turns from gas into liquid water. As the Sun rises, it takes a while for the moisture to turn back into gas, so droplets of water—or dew—collect on the cold leaf. Watch this happen at dawn . . .

Day is breaking, and the leaves of this garden are looking up to the sunrise.

The leaves have been cooled by the cold night air.

Moisture in the cold air turns into liquid and collects on the leaf as dew.

When the temperature drops, this dew can turn to ice—which we also call frost.

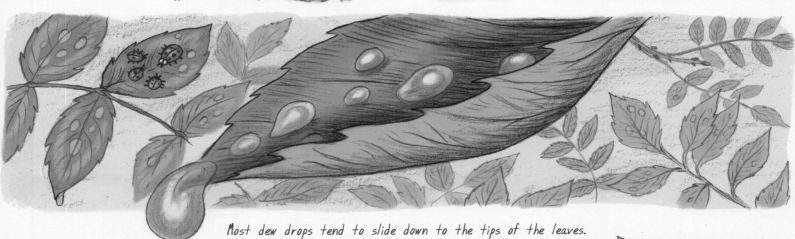

Most dew drops tend to slide down to the tips of the leaves.

A big droplet forms and falls off the leaf. DRIP!

The day has begun, and the leaf is nearly dry . . . until tomorrow.

➷ A BUTTERFLY ➶
EMERGES FROM A CHRYSALIS

You may have heard stories about a very hungry caterpillar munching on leaves before it becomes a beautiful butterfly— but what happens while it is inside its chrysalis?

A butterfly's chrysalis is a hard, protective case—like a moth's cocoon—which hides part of a complex process called metamorphosis. Inside, the caterpillar changes into a pupa, growing eyes, wings, legs, and other body parts.

Two weeks later, the silky chrysalis becomes see-through, revealing the creature's bright wings and antennae.

The day has come for the butterfly to make its way into the world and take flight! See this magical moment for a monarch butterfly, as she prepares to take the journey of a lifetime . . .

Hanging in her silent chrysalis, the butterfly's colorful wings can be seen moving inside.

As she emerges, her wings are small and crumpled. Her body is large and swollen with fluid.

First, she fuses together the parts of her mouth that form her proboscis: the tool she will use to drink nectar, a bit like a straw.

She then pumps fluid into her wings, making them grow wide and flat.

And just an hour or so after emerging from the chrysalis . . .

her wings are ready to use.

Usually within three or four hours, the butterfly will learn to fly. Her next job will be to find food, and then search for a mate to lay eggs of her own.

Her first stop on her long journey is lunch: nectar from a big, red flower nearby . . .

ꝏ A DUCK ꝏ
TEACHES HER DUCKLINGS TO SWIM

Ducklings have a great tool for swimming—big, webbed feet.

They spend about ten hours in their nest before their mothers lead them to a pond, lake, or stream nearby to test their water skills. Unlike adult ducks, ducklings do not yet have waterproof down (feathers). Their mother must cover them with oil from a gland near her tail to ensure the water doesn't make them too cold.

Together, they waddle out of their nest and make their way to the water as a group, ready for a meal. Directed by their mother, they are on the lookout for danger. Watch this brood of mallard ducklings follow their mother to the pond for their first steps into the water . . .

With all eight ducklings behind her, the mother duck waddles her way to the water, chatting as she goes.

At the water's edge, she shows her ducklings how to move slowly into the water, until it laps around her feet.

The ducklings listen and watch closely . . .

until she is floating on the water.

One by one, they follow her in.

Then, the mother duck dunks her head in the water to find food.

A duckling's webbed feet work wonders in water: as the web spreads out, it acts like a paddle, propelling the duckling along.

A duckling's bill is specially formed to help it forage in mud and sift food, such as insects and other small creatures, from the water.

When they are confident swimmers, this paddling of ducklings will follow their mother in a perfect line.

At two months old, the ducklings are big enough to fly—and will leave their nest to find new homes of their own.

A SPIDER WEAVES A WEB

Stronger than steel but light as a feather, a spider's silk web is a natural wonder.

For centuries, scientists have puzzled over what gives the silk web its strength and elasticity, but none have been able to create anything quite like it.

You just have to watch a web being made to understand that spiders are also skilled engineers.

Their silk-spinning organ—the spinneret—and eight legs make them quick workers. Most spiders begin as the Sun goes down for the day and finish two hours later. Used to catch breakfast and keep the spider out of harm's way, the web starts with a single silk line across a gap. Watch this common orb weaver in action as she weaves her web at sunset . . .

The spider starts by pulling silk from a gland using her fourth legs.

She adds to the strands with straight radial threads . . .

She catches a breeze and uses it to drift a silk line across a gap between two branches. Then she supports the line with approximately five extra threads.

and spiral threads.

Working her way inward, she uses her legs to create concentric circles,

ending with a central spiral of sticky silk.

Under the light of the Moon, the web stays mostly hidden from prey—like this unassuming fly who has flown into the web.

Sensing a vibration, the spider rushes out from center of the web . . .

and rapidly wraps her victim in silk, rotating it with her shorter middle legs.

Nom Nom!

Once the prey is secure, the spider gives the fly a bite and allows her venom to do its job.

When the web loses its stickiness, the spider eats the silk, taking back the protein. Now she's ready to create another one tomorrow.

11

THE DAWN CHORUS PERFORMS

It's still dark outside as the birds of the dawn chorus come together to welcome the light of day.

The dim light of dawn is not a good time to forage for breakfast, so until more light appears, the birds hold a singing contest.

Performing to defend their territories, their songs must also help them find a mate.

The best-fed males produce the strongest, most impressive songs. Not surprisingly, females choose these males as mates, since it's a sure sign that the father will help raise strong chicks. Depending on where you are in the world, the performers in this piece will vary.
See it here at dawn in an English garden...

About an hour before sunrise, robins and blackbirds begin the chorus.

These birds tend to be the first to sing because their larger eyes are more sensitive, allowing them to see in the early-morning light.

Their large eyes also help them search for tasty insects in the undergrowth.

The robin pierces the predawn song with a "cheerily, cheer up, cheerio" song.

The blackbird joins in the chorus, with a falling "cheer, cheer, cheer" and a rising "birdie, birdie, birdie."

Next to join in are the wrens and the warblers, who hide away from the night's cold but come out to sing at daybreak. "Churr, churr," they call.

Lastly, the seedeaters, such as sparrows, who have smaller eyes, join in the chorus when day is fully here.

These performers often leave gaps in their songs to listen for replies, which helps them work out where their rivals are and which females are paying attention to them.

And so, before cars turn the corner and the bus begins to move, the world is woken to the sound of birdsong.

A THUNDERSTORM
ON A SUMMER'S DAY

The sky darkens, the wind picks up, and clouds fill the sky,
as a low rumble announces the coming of a storm.

A tall, towering cloud breaks the summer Sun,
calling forth the rain as a flash of lightning is
answered by a low boom of thunder. A thunderstorm!

Thunder happens when a lightning bolt travels from the clouds to the ground, creating a partial vacuum. The air vibrates, causing sound waves that we can hear. We see lightning before we hear thunder because light travels faster than sound.
Nothing is more dramatic than the light show of lightning, wind and rain, and the clap of thunder . . .

We see the flash of lightning . . . then we hear the clap of thunder. CLAP!   And again. CLAP!

Lightning is a bolt of electricity. Ice crystals in a thundercloud bump into one another as they move around in the air. These collisions create an electric charge that builds up until— ZAP!—lightning strikes the ground.

With thunder comes rain.

It starts to pour . . .

Then the rain steadies, and pools of water form on the ground.

With light shining through the clouds, a calm evening is welcomed after the storm.

A SQUIRREL BURIES AN ACORN IN AUTUMN
AND DIGS IT UP AGAIN IN WINTER

Autumn is here, and as leaves fall to the ground, the grey squirrels of this parkland are collecting acorns to store up for the long winter.

The squirrel must pick the right acorn—not too big or too small. It should be on the verge of ripening so that it will be fully ready to eat in the winter, when the acorn can be detected by its strong scent. The squirrel must also find the perfect place to bury it—somewhere memorable and far enough away from other hungry squirrels.

Three months later, when the park is covered in snow, this squirrel will be back to dig up her acorn for supper. Watch her bury it, look for it, and nibble her tasty meal...

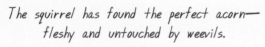

The squirrel has found the perfect acorn— fleshy and untouched by weevils.

Standing on a pile of red leaves, she digs a small hole in the soft earth and buries the acorn, patting down the earth with her forefeet.

Taking mental note of where she's left her acorn, she moves on to gather her next treat.

Scientists have watched squirrels burying and reburying their acorns. Some believe it helps them to remember where they have stored them; others think it's a tactic to help protect their stash.

Suspicious of thieves, squirrels will hide their nuts in difficult-to-reach places, such as under a bush or in a muddy patch.

Come winter, the squirrel returns to her patch under the oak tree.

Even under a foot of snow, the squirrel can smell her stash. She starts digging . . .

and keeps digging . . .

until her prized acorn is found.

She devours it and moves on to her next meal—another acorn or a stash of nuts, some of which will go home to her babies.

17

A BAT GOES HUNTING AT NIGHT

One of the world's best flyers is a mammal—not a bird—
who wakes up to begin his day at sunset.

Roosting during the day, bats
hang upside down in a position
that makes them ready for takeoff.
With broad, elastic wings, the long-eared
bat is thought to be one of the best flyers in
the world—able to catch prey midflight
as it glides through the forest at night.

All species of bat use a special type of hunting technique, called echolocation, to "see" things in the dark.
Long-eared bats are especially good at this, with sensitive hearing that allows them to pinpoint
an insect when sounds bounce back to them.

Roosting in his hole in a tree, the bat
wakes as night falls.

Shaking his wings out, he prepares to hunt.

Bats make high-pitched sounds and listen for the echo.
As they hear the sound bouncing off an object, they work
out its position. This is called echolocation.

The bat follows the movements of a moth nearby.

And before you can blink . . .

he has flown, gliding silently down from his tree.

He captures the moth midflight, and kills it with a single bite.

This dramatic moonlit scene might happen many more times tonight. Eating as he flies, the bat listens for his next meal . . .

A RAINBOW APPEARS

The Sun shines through the rain, bringing with it a bright, glistening rainbow.

Many people won't know that these magical beams of color are simply rays of light, split into colors that can only be seen if you are in the right place at the right time.

Depending on where you're watching it from, you'll see a different combination of colors: red light, for example, bends at a different angle than violet light. The best time to catch one is when the Sun is at its lowest-early in the morning or late in the day. So sit back and watch a rainbow light up a grey sky . . .

Find a dry spot after a rain shower, and make sure the Sun is behind you.

Look up and watch . . .

When sunlight passes through a raindrop, the white light bends (or refracts) and reflects off the inside of the raindrop. As it exits, this white light separates into many different colors . . .

An arc of colors appears before your eyes: red, orange, yellow, green, blue, indigo, and violet.

A magical rainbow, right in front of you!

As the rain clears, so will the rainbow . . . until next time.

A FOX EATS BERRIES FROM A BUSH

Foxes enjoy some of the best diets in the animal kingdom.

Expert hunters, foxes catch rabbits, mice, birds, frogs, and earthworms—and will rummage in trash cans for food if nothing can be found. But most of all, foxes love to raid a blackberry patch.

Fruit is a favorite food for the fox, who will go to any length to get its prize-climbing a tree or standing on its hind legs to reach berries high on a bush. A juicy, ripe blackberry at the end of summer is the best kind of treat for this young fox. Watch him as he goes berry hunting around his neighborhood . . .

The Sun has started to set on this garden's blackberry patch.

Spotting the berries on this bush, the young fox rears himself up on his hind legs.

Delicately, he uses his front paws to locate the ripest, juiciest berries.

With his long snout, he gently tips the berry to the top of his nose . . .

and with a SNAP!

CRUNCH,

and LICK, the berry is gone.

Foxes are omnivorous, which means that they eat both meat and plants.

And now, with darkness around him, it's time for the fox to go out and hunt for his main course . . .

23

A SNOWFLAKE FALLS

You may know that no two snowflakes are alike, but we can only understand why by watching how one is formed.

When a very cold water droplet freezes onto a pollen or dust particle in the sky, an ice crystal forms. As this ice crystal falls to the ground, more water freezes onto the original crystal, building new crystals—until a six-sided snowflake is made.

Each snowflake follows a different path to the ground, encountering slightly different weather conditions as it falls. So some look like icy prisms; others look like lace. But each one has six sides: the perfect shape for icy water to bond. A stellar dendrite begins like any other snowflake . . .

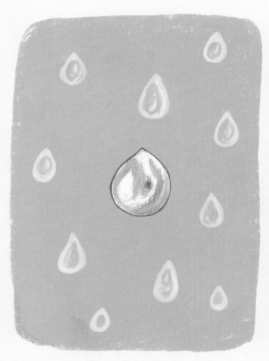

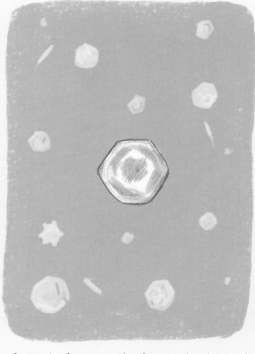

A water droplet turns to ice.

Crystals form on the frozen droplet and a prism is made, with six faces.

Ice grows faster at the corners of the prism, causing six branches to sprout.

The arms grow faster than the rest of the prism.

At around 5 degrees Fahrenheit, a stellar dendrite snowflake is formed.

As it reaches warmer air, new branches form on each branch . . . and so its journey continues, until it touches the ground.

Depending on the temperature and weather conditions that surround it, every snowflake will take on a different shape—like this selection here:

Stellar Dendrite
Formed in temperatures near 28°F or near 5°F

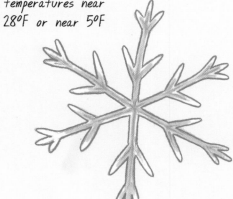

Needle
Formed in temperatures near 23°F

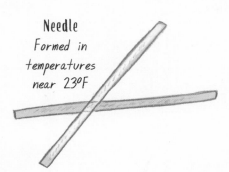

Fernlike Stellar Dendrite
Formed in temperatures near 5°F, high humidity

Stellar Plate
Formed in temperatures near 5°F, high humidity

Sectored Plate
Formed in temperatures near 5°F, less humidity

MAMA AND DADA BIRDS
FEED THEIR BABIES

After hatching, these baby birds don't open their eyes for five whole days.

Hatched from an egg, these babies arrive with bulging eyes and pink skin—and a gaping beak, ready for food. For the first few days, these babies will eat partly digested food from their parents.

On day five, mama and dada will feed them earthworms that have been broken up into small mouthfuls. But soon, these babies will be eating worms and insects all on their own. As a soft layer of feathers grows around the babies' bodies, their appetites also grow. Watch them grow here . . .

Five tiny nestlings hatch from their eggs, calling for the sixth to appear.

Some time later that morning, she arrives!

As soon as she emerges, she opens her beak wide. Eyes closed, she waits for food.

Eggs that are laid in nests are sometimes white or pale blue in color so that parents can find them more easily.

Mama and dada take turns to hunt and feed . . .

coming back each time with mouthfuls of worms to share with the nestlings.

Even though they can't see, babies will feel their parents land on the side of the nest and hear their calls.

The feast continues for about two weeks, during which time the babies will eat hundreds of earthworms!

And soon, they'll be big enough to stretch their wings . . .

and leave the nest in search of a mate and a nest to make their own.

✵ A HONEYBEE HIVE GETS TO WORK ✵

A honeybee hive is home to as many as 40,000 bees, living and working together like clockwork.

Each colony has one queen bee, several hundred male drones and thousands of female workers. The queen lays the eggs, the drones mate with the queen, and the workers do everything else.

Throughout their lives, worker bees take on different jobs to make sure that the hive survives. Visiting up to 2,000 flowers each day to collect nectar, these workers also do all the housekeeping; feed the queen, drones, and young larvae; collect pollen and nectar; and make wax. Because they work so hard, they only live for a short time: just six weeks in the summer. Watch them get to work on this spring morning . . .

They clean. *Every cell in the hive must be cleaned before it is reused for storing honey or new eggs.*

They feed the hive. *Foraging nectar from flowers and plants, they come back to the hive over and over to deliver food.*

They make wax. At around twelve days old, wax flakes begin to appear on the bees' bellies. This wax is used to build new wax cells and cap the ones storing honey.

They guard the hive. Every bee that visits the hive is checked by a leading worker bee to make sure they are part of the colony. She may also sound the alarm if a gang of wasps is nearby!

They make honey. Nectar is more than three-quarters water, so once it is brought back to the hive, the bees dry it out by passing it from mouth to mouth, before storing it in wax cells. Then, they beat their wings to further dry the nectar into honey.

They dance. Honeybees can't talk, so they communicate with movement. When they find a great source of nectar, they perform a waggle dance, showing other worker bees where to find it.

And finally ... they sleep. Even the toughest worker bees need five to eight hours a day of undisturbed rest.

THE MOON WAXES . . . AND WANES

The brightest light in the night sky is never the same from one evening to the next.

Each night, the Moon appears to have changed shape. In fact, it's just going through its monthly journey around Earth.

As the Moon travels, the Sun lights up different parts of it, which makes it look like it's changing shape-growing, or waxing, and shrinking, or waning.

The Moon takes around four weeks to complete its journey around Earth. As it travels, it goes through eight different phases, called a lunar cycle. Look out your window tonight. Can you tell where the Moon is on its journey?

Day 1. New Moon: This happens at the start of the lunar cycle, when the Moon is directly between the Earth and the Sun.

During the new Moon phase, the Moon looks dark to us because the side of the Moon facing us receives no sunlight.

Day 4. Waxing crescent: As the Moon continues to move, more and more of it is illuminated by the Sun. The Moon looks like a crescent under the starry sky.

Day 7. Half Moon: On this night, we might think we can see half of the Moon from Earth, but in reality, three-quarters of it is still hidden by darkness.

Day 10.
Waxing gibbous:
Slowly, more than half of the lit portion of the Moon is revealed to us, and it gets fuller and fuller each day.

We only ever see one side of the Moon, because it spins at the same speed as its journey around the Earth.

Day 14. Full Moon: Halfway through the cycle, we see all of the Moon's face lit up.

The Moon itself doesn't actually give off any light—"moonlight" is actually the Sun's light reflected off the Moon's surface.

Day 18. Waning gibbous: By now, the lit-up portion of the Moon starts to decrease, or wane, from one day to the next.

Day 22. Last quarter: Only half of the lit-up portion of the Moon is visible.

Day 26. Waning crescent: Toward the end of the cycle, the Moon looks like a crescent once more, slowly disappearing each evening . . .

and we're back to the new Moon phase, when our brightest night-light seems hidden from sight, ready for a brand-new cycle to begin.

31

AN OCEAN WAVE FORMS, CRESTS, AND BREAKS

Water in the ocean is always moving. Beneath the surface, water moves in currents, some of which run hundreds of feet deep.

Most often, waves are caused by the wind moving across the water's surface. The energy of the wind makes the water whirl and swirl.

As the wave moves closer to the shore, the bottom of the wave slows down, dragging along the ocean floor. As the top part of the wave keeps moving and overtakes the bottom, a crest starts to spill forward and the wave breaks. Watch a wave form on a windy day at the beach . . .

1. Waves begin when wind blows across the water's surface.

2. The top layers of the water move more quickly than the bottom layers.

3. The water starts to move in a circular motion.

4. This motion causes crests to appear. The higher the wave, the taller the crests!

The wave gets bigger as it nears the shoreline. As the seabed gets shallower, the wave is pushed upward.

The top of the wave moves faster than the bottom, and it topples forward . . . and breaks!

The tallest wave ever measured was 1,719 feet high at Lituya Bay, Alaska.

And so the circle of waves continues. These surfers have waited for this windy day to catch the perfect ride.

A TADPOLE BECOMES A FROG

Tadpoles begin their lives as eggs in water. The female frog lays eggs and the male fertilizes them—sometimes up to 1,500 eggs at a time!

Under the careful watch of their father, these fertilized eggs stick together and bob on the water's surface.

Surrounding each egg, a clear jelly protects the tadpole as it begins to change into a frog—a journey called metamorphosis. Watch the common frog transform over at least 84 days: one of the longest and most magical metamorphosis journeys in the animal kingdom . . .

Between 6 and 21 days after fertilization, the egg hatches, and a tiny fishlike creature called a tadpole appears.

The tadpole stays inside his egg and feeds on the yolk for a couple of days, until he's strong enough to swim and feed on algae and pond weed.

After about four weeks, the tadpole develops gills inside his body. He breathes by taking in water through his mouth and passing it over his gills.

Common frog tadpoles are black when they hatch but become speckly as they grow.

Between six and nine weeks, the tadpole grows hind legs, and his head begins to take shape. He will also start to eat other creatures, such as small pond insects.

At the end of the ninth week, the tadpole starts to look like a frog, with front legs—but with a long tail.

Over ten to twelve weeks, the tadpole will absorb the tail back into his body. Soon, it will be a froglet.

It still takes the little froglet two weeks to grow into an adult frog. In a few years, the frog will look for a mate to fertilize her eggs!

BLUEBELLS
TRANSFORM A WOODLAND

There's something magical about a woodland bursting with bluebells.

Heralding the start of spring, bluebells cover the forest with a dazzling blue carpet of flowers, transforming a woodland into another world.

It can take four or five years to grow bluebells from a seed, but once they are up, bees, hoverflies, and butterflies take their first drink of spring nectar from these flowers. The common bluebell is a national treasure in England, where more than half of the world's bluebells live. Because they grow so slowly from seed to flower, bluebells are thought to be a sign of an ancient forest, some dating back 400 years . . .

Bluebells start their journey upward in the new year.

January: initial growth	February: shoots appear	March: leaves develop	April/May: first flowers!	June: seeds set	July: dormancy (deep sleep)

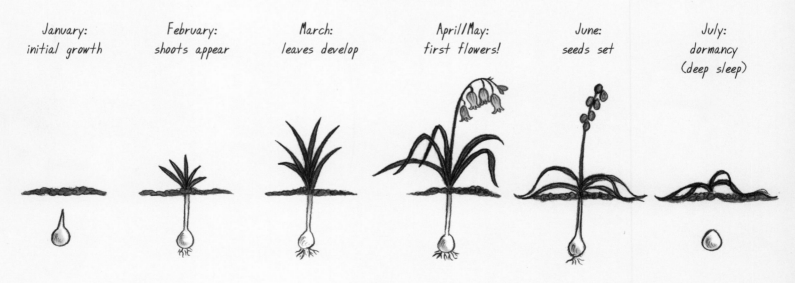

They soak up the early spring sunshine and store it in their bulbs underground.

See the common bluebell transform an English woodland before your eyes . . .

The daffodils have come and gone, so it's time for the bluebells to ring in the springtime.

By late spring, the forest is a carpet of blue. In a couple of weeks it starts to fade, and the bluebells die back.

Even under the new year's snow, next year's bluebells are beginning to make their way out into the world. When the snow clears, a bluebell's first shoots appear. And so the journey continues . . .

⚜ A MOLE ⚜
TOPS UP HIS STORE OF EARTHWORMS

A garden mole may look harmless, but it has an enormous appetite.

A mole gets so hungry, in fact, that it has to eat nearly its own bodyweight in earthworms each day.

This means that much of a mole's time is spent digging tunnels in search of food, using its big paddle-shaped paws to find its way underground.

There, a mole will dig a special chamber at the end of each tunnel for its store of earthworms. It might store up to 470 earthworms in these chambers, where they lie helpless after a single mole bite to the neck. Watch one little mole complete his daily work...

This mole has been busy looking for worms this morning. At this garden's surface, he pops his head out...

and spies a worm wriggling in the dirt.

CHOMP!

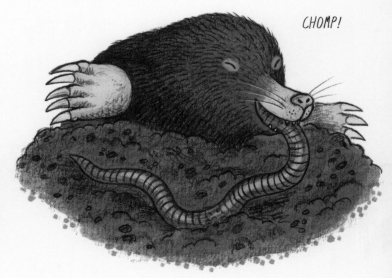

The saliva in his mouth has a poison in it, which leaves the worm unable to move.

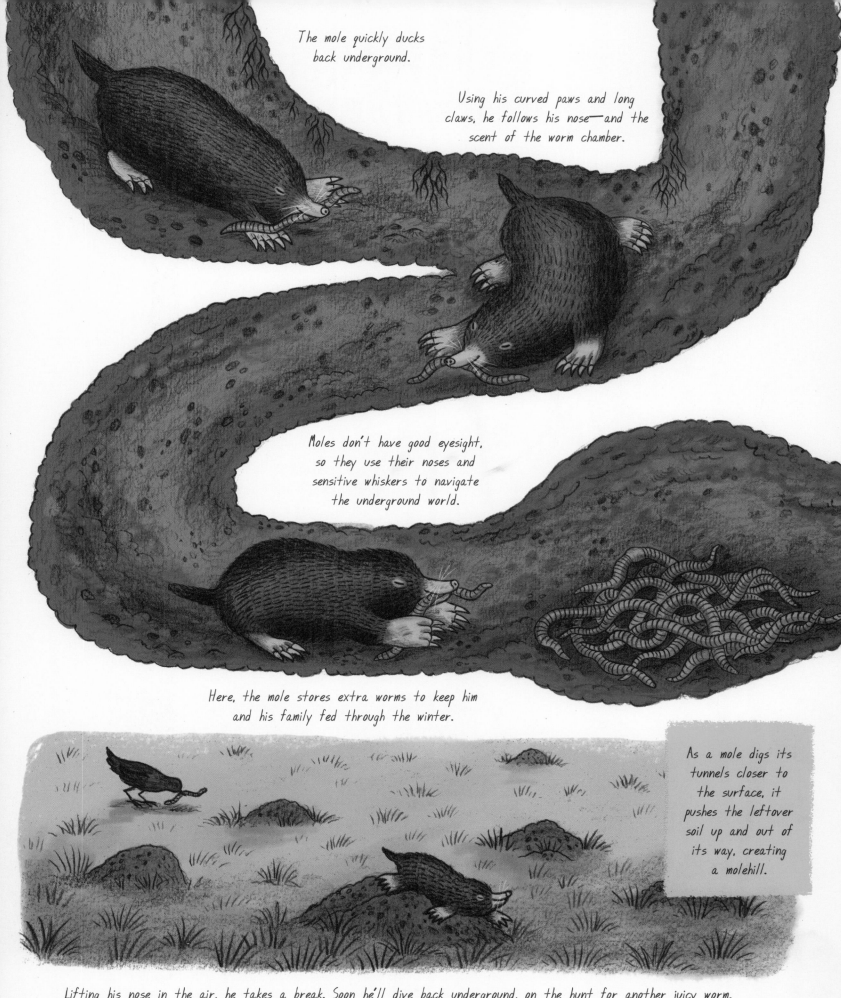

The mole quickly ducks
back underground.

Using his curved paws and long
claws, he follows his nose—and the
scent of the worm chamber.

Moles don't have good eyesight,
so they use their noses and
sensitive whiskers to navigate
the underground world.

Here, the mole stores extra worms to keep him
and his family fed through the winter.

As a mole digs its
tunnels closer to
the surface, it
pushes the leftover
soil up and out of
its way, creating
a molehill.

Lifting his nose in the air, he takes a break. Soon he'll dive back underground, on the hunt for another juicy worm.

A SUNFLOWER
TRACKS THE SUN

Why do sunflowers face the Sun?

Young sunflowers want to be as big as possible and attract as many insects as they can to help spread their pollen. Scientists have discovered that a sunflower is most attractive to bees when the flower is warm—so it has developed a unique ability to turn to face the Sun!

This process is called heliotropism, and is a bit like a human's circadian rhythm—or the internal body clock that helps us sleep at night and wake in the morning. Here, a young sunflower faces east to greet the Sun, then slowly turns west as the Sun moves across the sky. Let's watch it happen over a 24-hour period . . .

Dawn has come, and the young sunflower has waited hours for this moment.

Lifting its head, it catches the first glimpse of morning sunshine.

Good morning! Facing its source of light and heat, the sunflower begins to move with the Sun.

In the morning, its stem is bent slightly toward the east, where the Sun rises.

At lunchtime, it faces upward as it slowly turns to the west, tracking the Sun.

At sunset, the sunflower has bent right over toward the west, where it will stay until the Sun goes down. At night, it will bend toward the east once more, ready for sunrise.

When it gets old, this sunflower will stop moving.

Heated up by the Sun, it awaits a visit from insects, which spread its pollen . . . helping make brand new sunflowers!

A GAME OF CAT AND MOUSE

Cats may look cute and cuddly, but they are natural hunters.

Almost from the day it is born, a kitten is taught by its mother how to spot the tiniest movement of a mouse, using its amazing eyesight.

But a mouse has its own defences, helping it stay alert to a pouncing cat. It has a fantastic nose that can smell the saliva of a hungry feline. One sniff, and the mouse scurries away, out of sight.

Scientists have discovered that a protein produced in a cat's saliva sets off a special sensory organ in the mouse, called the vomeronasal organ-causing the mouse to flee.

Who will win this game of cat and mouse?

It's a lovely sunny morning and the cat is cleaning her paws.

All cats, from tabby to tiger, eat lots of animal protein to stay fit and strong.

She picks up the faintest noise in the garden wall and turns her nose toward it, to catch a whiff of scent.

A little mouse is making her way through the long garden grass when she spots a movement ahead.

In a panic, she runs ahead and tips over the garden pot. SMASH!

The cat usually likes to hunt by stealth, remaining unseen . . . but the mouse's cover is blown.

The cat races over and pounces right on top of the flower pot, just as the mouse scrambles away . . .

and disappears under the shed. The cat may be faster than the little mouse, but she can't fit into tiny spaces.

She will wait there with extreme patience until the mouse reappears, and then—

POUNCE!

"Miaoooow!" The cat cries as the mouse escapes, running rings around her captor. And so the cycle begins again . . .

A SHOOTING STAR
LIGHTS UP THE NIGHT SKY

Have you ever caught sight of a bright shooting star?

These traveling balls of light are not actually stars, but pieces of rock or debris that hit Earth's atmosphere from space.

In space, there are lots of bits of rock floating around. This rock moves so quickly that it heats up and burns like a star as it moves through our atmosphere. Astronomers call these pieces of rock meteors, and they mostly burn up before they reach the ground. Whatever they are, there's no reason not to make a wish on one. Let's watch them here on a clear, starry night . . .

Asteroids break up when they hit the Earth's atmosphere. The broken pieces are called meteors.

The moment a meteor hits our atmosphere, it compresses air particles, which begins to heat up . . .

Shooting stars are extremely fast, reaching speeds of more than 100,000 miles per hour.

glowing and burning brightly.

The heat burns up, or vaporizes, the meteor, creating what we see as a shooting star. Now its time to make a wish!

A SNAKE SHEDS ITS SKIN

Every two to three weeks, a young snake sheds its skin. All animals shed their skin—even humans—but it's hard to see it happening in a single moment.

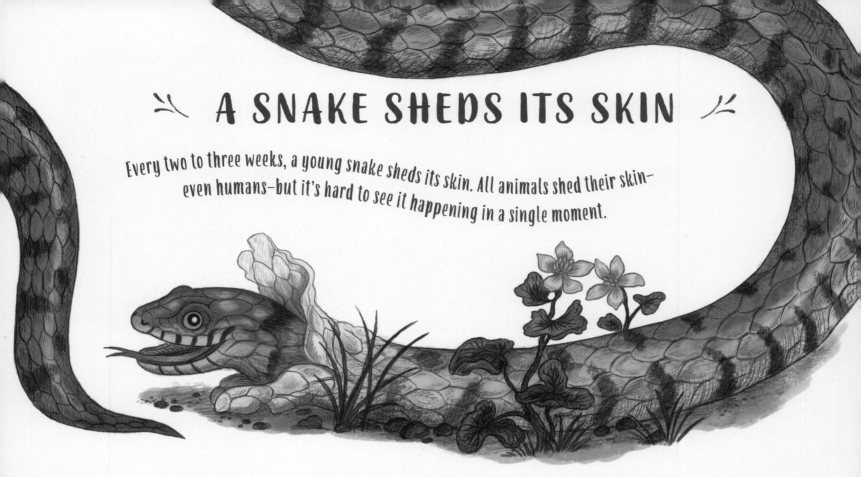

A snake loses its skin in one long piece, as if it were taking off a sock.

As a snake grows, its skin doesn't, and so it must shed its current layer and remove parasites or bugs that have attached themselves to it. Scientists call this process ecdysis, or molting. The snake needs its new skin immediately, so it grows this layer underneath its current one. As it gets older, the snake will only shed its skin two or three times a year. Let's see how this young snake transforms his outer layer . . .

This young snake's skin has begun to look a little rough, and his eyes a little cloudy.

Spotting a pond nearby, he slithers in.
The water will help loosen the old skin and allow it to come off in one piece.

Emerging from the water . . .   the snake spots a hard rock nearby and slithers over to it.

He rubs his head on the rock until his skin tears a little.

Slithering through the tear, he begins to make his way out of his skin. The whole process can take less than an hour.

If you are lucky enough to find a skin, you might see that it's turned inside out— as if the snake had taken its sock off.

So watch out for a skin on your next walk near a pond . . . just hours ago, it may have housed a friendly snake!

MUSHROOMS GROW IN A FOREST

You may be surprised to know that 90 percent of the plants in a forest depend on mushrooms.

They break down wood and recycle plant food back into soil—the ground in which trees and plants grow.

A mushroom's complex system of roots, called a mycelium, stretches out underground, searching for water and food. Unlike plants, mushrooms don't get their food from the Sun. Instead, they make their home in a dark, moist environment—such as this woodland. Watch a wood blewit bloom as the autumn months approach . . .

A young mushroom's life begins when a mature mushroom spreads its spores—tiny seeds too small for the human eye to see.

These spores fall to the ground, where they take root.

When two or more "roots" meet, a mycelium is formed.

After about 14 days, a fruit body begins to form on the mycelium.

The fruit body of the mushroom pushes its head above the soil's surface . . .

up, up . . .

and out! Fanning its umbrella, the mushroom is fully grown.

The red fly agaric mushroom (also called a toadstool) may look magical—but it is actually poisonous.

When the frost comes, this mushroom will start to mature, and its edges will become frayed and turn upward.

As the mushroom begins to break down into the soil, its spores disperse, and the lifecycle of a mushroom begins again.

⍋ A SPECTACULAR SUNSET DESCENDS ⍋

The day is nearly done, but not before a bright orange sunset lights up the sky.

Light from the Sun's rays is white but consists of seven different colors that we cannot always see—
violet, indigo, blue, green, yellow, orange, and red.

At sunset, our position on the planet is slowly rotating away from the Sun, so sunlight has to travel a long way through Earth's atmosphere for us to see it. Most colors, like blue and green, are scattered away before they reach Earth. But the colors with the longest wavelengths—red and orange—are able to reach our eyes more easily. Go on a walk, climb a hill, or just stand in your garden to watch tonight's sunset . . .

It's been a bright, autumnal day.

The Sun begins to travel down toward the horizon . . .

. . . but not before it makes the sky a brilliant orange.

All of nature stops to marvel at the wondrous colors—pinks, oranges, and reds.

Creatures of the night come out to watch, too: a little fox, a mouse, and a bat emerge to see the bright performance . . .

until the Sun dips far beneath the horizon, and is gone.

For the next ten hours, darkness sets in . . . waiting for the warm colors of the sunrise tomorrow.

A SNAIL LEAVES A TRAIL

A silvery trail, glistening on the path ahead of you, gives you a clue . . . a snail has been here!

Snails are part of a group of animals called gastropods. The name means "stomach foot" because a snail's body is like one long foot with a mouth on one end.

Snails produce slime, or mucus, which comes from a special gland on the front of their foot. This mucus is their secret power—it helps them stick to whatever surface they're on, whether it be a footpath, a rock, or a tree. It also protects them from the Sun's harmful rays, and in dry weather, it helps the snail curl up inside its moist shell. Watch this garden snail produce slime on his journey around the garden . . .

It's a rainy summer's day—perfect for this little snail.

He mostly hunts at night for plants and algae. But when a slight shower appears, he heads out to forage for garden scraps . . .

over a rock . . .

along the garden path . . .

. . . and up a tree.

What an active snail!

If the weather is too dry, snails will retreat to the safety of their slimy, moist shells for a little nap. This is called estivation.

Then back down again . . . to his little mossy home next to the garden pond.

When the rain stops and the sunshine comes out, the little snail curls into his shell. But not before leaving a trace of his daily journey for a young spotter to find.

A TREE'S LEAVES
CHANGE COLOR . . . AND FALL

Autumn is here, welcomed by streets filled with orange, yellow, and red trees.

At this time of year, the days get shorter and colder, and there is less sunshine. Leaves change color and fall to the ground.

Without long hours of sunlight, leaves stop producing chlorophyll—the chemical that keeps them green during the spring and summer, and helps them make food from the sunshine. Instead, they start using food that has been stored away for this time of year. In doing so, their green color fades, revealing the bright yellows, oranges, and reds of autumn. So take a walk in this park and watch these leaves turn . . .

In spring, the trees begin to blossom.

A green pigment, chlorophyll, dominates the leaves, turning them a brilliant green.

As the days warm up and become longer, the leaves turn sunlight into food.

Plants, algae, and bacteria are the only living things able to turn sunlight into food. This process is called photosynthesis.

When autumn shows its face, the tree's leaves stop making chlorophyll and focus instead on using up their stores of food, or glucose.

As their chloropyll fades, the other colors of the leaves begin to show through.

Bright yellows . . . oranges . . . and finally a brilliant red.

As the stems of the leaves weaken, they fall from the trees . . .

into big piles!

Winter is here and the tree rests. But not for long. Even now, the first signs of spring can be seen.

A SPARROW TAKES A BATH

Tree sparrows are some of the world's best bathers.

Meeting together in groups, they gather around a birdbath to splash and clean themselves.

There are a number of ways that sparrows take a bath. In dry climates, they bathe in dust to get rid of excess oil from their feathers as they shake the dust away. In cities and towns, sparrows will usually find a source of water to make sure their feathers are properly cleaned.

Join them here, for their morning bath routine...

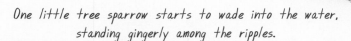

One little tree sparrow starts to wade into the water, standing gingerly among the ripples.

Fluffing up her feathers, she spreads her wings wide, ready to dip her belly in the water . . .

She rapidly flicks her wings in and out, showering water all around her.

Splash! Dipping her beak in, she throws her head backward, dousing her back with a cooling spray.

She elevates her back feathers to ensure they catch the shower of water.

She might perform this sequence up to five times during this one bath, as others join in.

Once suitably wet, the sparrow dries herself by vibrating her wings and tail, and ruffling her feathers.

Found near the base of its tail, a sparrow's preen gland produces an oily, waxy substance that it uses to coats its feathers.

Bath time comes to an end with the birds preening themselves, rearranging their feathers and coating them in oil from their preen glands. This makes sure they stay waterproof . . . until their next bath!

A CLOUD FORMS

Today brings a beautiful blue sky—a perfect canvas to fill with white, fluffy clouds.

Most clouds form when warm air rises from the ground into the atmosphere.

There, it cools down. As it cools, tiny, invisible molecules of water in the air, called water vapor, clump together into larger water droplets or ice crystals, in a process called condensation. More and more droplets collect . . . and a cloud is made.
So, let's look up, and watch a cumulus cloud form . . .

It is midmorning on a clear day, and sunshine warms the ground.

As the air around the ground heats up, it rises. In the atmosphere, it expands, and then cools.

When millions of these droplets collect, a cumulus cloud forms.

58

Clouds are an important part of our weather system. There are ten basic types, each of which forms under different weather conditions:

Cumulonimbus clouds, which tower across the low, middle, and upper atmosphere, resemble large cumulus clouds.

Cumulonimbus

Cirrus

Cirrocumulus

Cirrostratus

High-level clouds form at around 20,000 feet high.
Cirrus look like thin, wispy strands of cloud that streak across the sky.
Cirrocumulus are white rows of cloud that can look like the scales of a fish.
Cirrostratus cover the whole sky and are see-through.

Altostratus

Altocumulus

Middle clouds form between 6,500 and 20,000 feet high.
Altocumulus, the most common clouds in the middle atmosphere, look like the wool of a sheep.
Altostratus are thin sheets of cloud that the Sun shines through.

Nimbostratus

Stratocumulus

Cumulus

Stratus

Low-level clouds form below 6,500 feet high.
Cumulus are white, fluffy clouds that form on clear days.
Nimbostratus are a dark grey layer of cloud that blocks the Sun.
Stratus look a bit like fog, and are usually grey.
Stratocumulus are low, puffy grey or white clouds that show patches of blue sky in between.

Each day brings with it a new sky . . . and new clouds.
Go outside and see which ones you can spot today!

59

A CHICK HATCHES
FROM AN EGG

For something so light, the shell of a chick's
egg is actually very strong.

Cased between walls of calcium
carbonate—the same thing that
pearls are made of—a hatchling must
work hard to break its way out of an egg.

Using its egg tooth—a tiny hornlike tooth at the tip of its upper beak—it chisels away at the inside layers of the
egg until, eventually, a break, or pip, in the shell is made. Then, the chick may rest for six to twelve hours while
its lungs adapt, before it continues to hatch. Watch this extraordinary event occur as the mother hen looks on . . .

This little hatchling has been incubating
inside her egg for about 21 days.

When she needs more oxygen, she uses her egg tooth to begin
to break into the air cell at the blunt end of the egg.

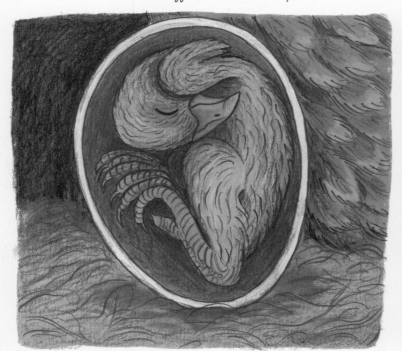

Until now, the chick embryo has absorbed all the
oxygen she needs through the shell's pores.

This is the start of a process called pipping.

This pocket of air provides enough extra oxygen to keep the hatchling alive—sometimes for days—until she can continue to punch a hole through the outside shell of the egg.

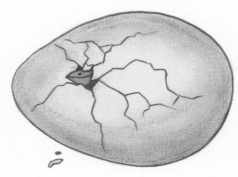

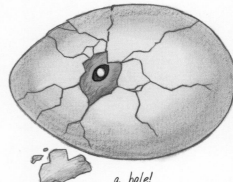

Punch . . .

crack . . .

a hole!

The hatchling rests while her lungs get used to her new environment.

Once rested, she uses her egg tooth to chip the shell many, many more times, until she can push her way out.

Pop! There she goes.

Out crawls the little chick, ready to be fed. Luckily, the mother hen is waiting nearby to greet her.

CHERRY BLOSSOMS
FALL TO THE GROUND

Nothing says springtime like a blossoming cherry tree.

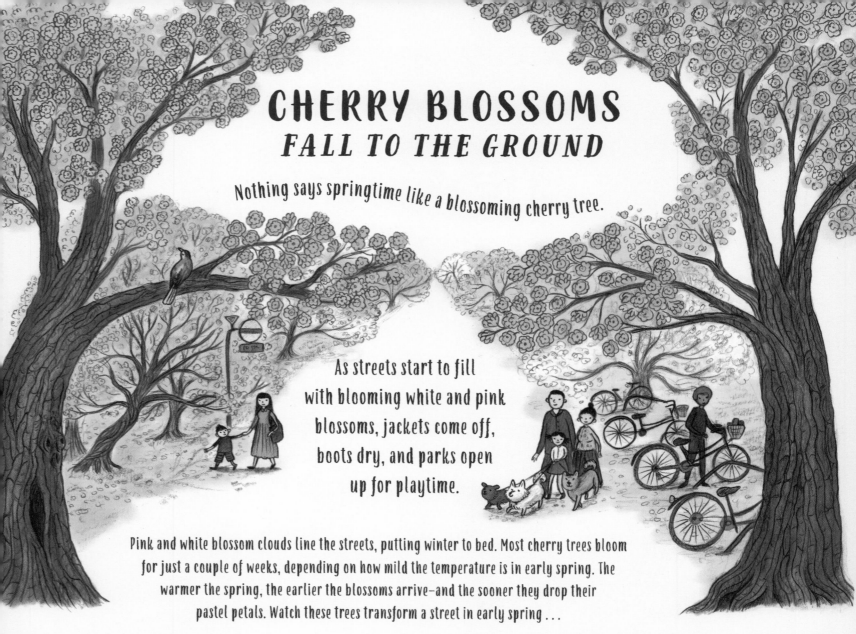

As streets start to fill with blooming white and pink blossoms, jackets come off, boots dry, and parks open up for playtime.

Pink and white blossom clouds line the streets, putting winter to bed. Most cherry trees bloom for just a couple of weeks, depending on how mild the temperature is in early spring. The warmer the spring, the earlier the blossoms arrive—and the sooner they drop their pastel petals. Watch these trees transform a street in early spring . . .

Winter is here, and the leaves of this cherry blossom tree have yet to grow. But tiny buds are beginning to show their faces . . .

As milder temperatures arrive, tiny florets appear—their closed, white petals still hiding from the world.

Over the next couple of days, they begin to open . . .

flower by flower . . .

until they puff . . . and bloom.

Cherry blossoms inspire festivals all around the world— particularly in Japan and America.

For a couple of weeks, these blossoms shine bright, filling the grey street with blooms.

As the trees start to shed their blossoms, they cover the ground with a blanket of pink . . .

and white.

Spring draws us into its warmth with a carpet of petals, before the gentle wind sweeps it away.

Until next year . . .

WEAVER ANTS BUILD A NEST

Weaver ants are some of nature's best team players.

When the time comes to build a home, each ant plays a vital role, as they work together to create a dwelling made from leaves.

To secure the leaves into a cone-shape that hides them from predators, these ants do something seen nowhere else in nature—they use their own food, larval silk, to stick the leaves together. It takes many ants, and extraordinary teamwork, to build their home over a 24-hour period. Marvel at their ingenuity as the building work starts at the top of a tree canopy . . .

Climbing his way up into the canopy, a single ant looks for the largest and most elastic leaves.

He calls to his workmate, who climbs over him. Grasping the newcomer by its waist, the ant edges closer to the leaf. It happens again . . . and again, until a whole chain of ants form a bridge to the leaf.

Colonies of weaver ants can be very large, made up of more than half a million workers.

He finds one, but it is just out of reach.

Like a construction crane, the weaver ants pull the leaf
downward to meet another leaf.

Holding the edges together, they sit and wait . . .

while another set of weavers does the same with
another pair of leaves.

Evening comes and more workers arrive from
nearby nests, carrying young larvae.

The weavers tap the
heads of the larvae,
which tells the larvae
to release the silk from
their saliva glands.

As the silk appears, the weaver ants use
it to glue the leaves together.

Hours later, the new home is finished, and the ants
move on to find another day's work . . .

FIDDLEHEADS
UNFURL IN THE SUNSHINE

Spring is a moment when nature unfurls,
and no plant shows this more than the fiddlehead.

Woken up by the spring sunshine, the buds of this fern have been
born out of spores that a mature fern has dropped to the ground.

Finding moisture-rich soil, a spore grows into something called a gametophyte, which is a heart-shaped plant. Within this plant, a sperm and an egg meet . . . and a young fern is formed. The tightly coiled head of the fern pushes through the soil and out of the earth, revealing its many fronds (leaves) as it grows. Watch one unfurl here . . .

Fossil records show that ferns have been on Earth for more than 360 million years!

The fiddlehead makes its way bravely up through the soil, pushing other plants and roots to one side.

Slowly turning its head toward the sky, it begins to stretch outward and upward.

As it grows, its fronds
fan outward.

outward and up.

unfurling . . .

Uncurling . . .

Finally, the very top of the head begins to
uncurl as the fern takes shape . . .
and opens.

The fern is now free to hang gently, fully open.
Drinking in the woodland's water-rich soil,
we wait as other ferns begin to unfurl nearby.

A MOSQUITO
MAKES A NARROW ESCAPE

The bothersome mosquito may seem like a pest,
but before you swat it, think about its place in nature.

Mosquitoes are important pollinators for plants, helping to
transfer pollen from flower to flower as they search for nectar.

Mosquitoes also act as food for
creatures such as birds, frogs, and fish.
And they won't bother you without reason!

In fact, it's only the females of the species who try to
bite humans, using their snout, or proboscis, to suck
our blood. In need of protein to reproduce, female
mosquitoes feed on both humans and nectar, while
males just feed on nectar. See one make a narrow
escape on this bright, sunny day . . .

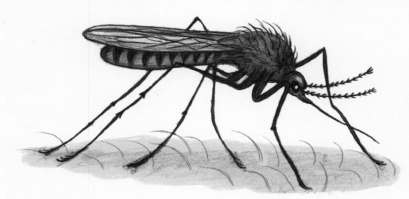

This female mosquito is hungry. She finds her meal by sensing
the body heat and carbon dioxide of a human nearby.

Carbon dioxide
is in the air we
breathe out.

Found her! Silently, she makes her move . . .

landing undetected on a human arm.

She takes a long drink.
SLURP!

"Ouch!"

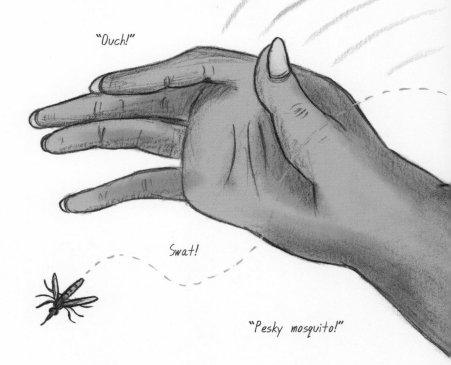

Swat!

"Pesky mosquito!"

In the blink of an eye, the mosquito gets what she came for.
But just then . . .

There are roughly 3,500 species of mosquito, but only around 200 of these need human or animal blood to survive.

She makes a narrow escape and goes off in search of nectar . . . a much more friendly meal!

A WOODPECKER
GETS TO WORK

Can you hear a fast, rhythmic "tap, tap, tap"?

A woodpecker in a nearby tree is digging for its dinner!

Gripping the tree trunk with its claws, the woodpecker props itself up on a branch with its stiff tail. Gathering speed, it pecks away at the branch, sensing a meal of worms or bugs inside.

Its long bill sharpens as it pecks—20 times per second—and with such force that its brain has to be protected from damage with a special skull. This skull is partly made up of spongy bone, and is also surrounded by the bird's long tongue, which gives it extra cushioning. Once a hole is made in a tree, the woodpecker sticks its long, sticky tongue inside to catch a meal. Let's watch it in action . . .

A woodpecker also uses this pecking motion to attract a mate and mark its territory.

A hungry little woodpecker spies a young tree and hops over to it.

Using his claws to climb, he finds a branch and turns around to inspect the trunk.

Hearing a movement inside the trunk, the woodpecker starts to peck . . .

and peck . . .

scattering the bark of the tree as he works.

Woodpeckers may peck up to 12,000 times in a single day.

The drilling motion finally creates a small hole.

In with his tongue! The woodpecker wastes no time in gathering his meal.

A long, sticky worm is lunch today.

Satisfied with his find, the woodpecker finishes his food and gently makes his way down the tree.

Still hungry, he looks for a spot to dig for his next meal . . .

A SEA STAR SHUFFLES
ACROSS THE OCEAN FLOOR

One of the most unusual aquatic animals isn't actually a fish.

Sea stars, also known as starfish, belong to a group of animals called marine invertebrates, which means that they lack a vertical spine.

Named after their starlike shape, these animals live in shallow waters and shuffle back and forth across the ocean floor using hundreds or thousands of tubes on their feet. Like miniature suction caps, these tubes also allow a sea star to gather hard-to-reach food, like clams or oysters, and hold their shells open while the star's sack-like stomach emerges to swallow its prey. Watch this incredible event take place on a nearby beach . . .

The sea star cannot see the clam shell, but it can smell it—by sensing chemicals released by the clam in the shallows.

Shuffling its way across the ocean floor, the sea star locates the clam and climbs on top of it.

A clam is very hard to open, but this sea star is hungry and will find a way!

Using its tiny suction-cup feet, it pulls on the clam's lid . . .

and pulls . . .

and pulls . . .

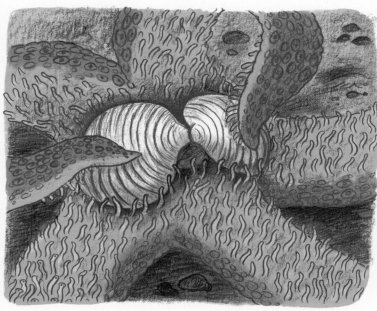 

until—POP!—the shell opens.

In an instant, the sea star pushes one of its two stomachs into the clam's shell . . . and begins to eat the clam.

Pulling its stomach and the liquified clam back inside, the sea star continues to digest its meal. It's time to feast!

A DRAGONFLY
PERFORMS AN AERIAL SHOW

Dragonflies are some of the best flyers in the world.

You may have spotted one hovering over a garden pond or
gliding along a local canal on a summer's evening.

For more than 300 million years, these insects have flown almost silently forward, backward, and upside down through our skies . . . even looping the loop. With two sets of wings, a dragonfly can move forward at a speed of up to 30 miles per second, hovering and accelerating in any direction they wish. Unlike other flying creatures, whose wings move backward and forward, dragonflies push their wings downward and backward—and then upward and forward. This type of flapping helps them use the air's drag to stay aloft. Let's watch this in action . . .

It's a lovely summer's morning, and this dragonfly is about to head out in search of food.

Spotting a mosquito, he takes off in an instant.

He flies silently behind it, ready to pounce.

Lining up his body
in the flight direction
of the mosquito,
the dragonfly does
a loop . . .

Dragonflies have
large, round eyes
that are made
up of thousands
of smaller eyes.
This allows
them to see in
many different
directions.

and starts to hover backward, beneath the mosquito's blind spot.

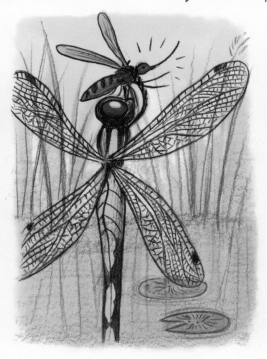

In a millisecond, the mosquito
is caught . . .

and grasped tightly by the
dragonfly's legs.

The dragonfly eats its meal
midflight—fast food on the go!

WATER LILIES
OPEN ON A POND

The calm waters of a still pond are the perfect home for a family of water lilies.

The wide, fanlike leaves, or lily pads, of the plant float on the water's surface, creating a resting spot for local wildlife like frogs, dragonflies, and leaf beetles.

Throughout the day, the flowers of the plant begin to open in the warmth of the Sun: their white petals brightening the dark, muddy surface of a pond.

With a center of yellow stamens, each flower lasts only for a few days, attracting bees and flies to feast on the plant's pollen. Watch the wildlife feed, rest, and play here over the course of a single day . . .

Morning has broken, and the water lilies of this pond are waking up to the sunshine.

A family of frogs enjoys the floating lily pads of the pond . . .

and a hungry water vole pops his head up to feed on the tasty green leaves.

A water lily's roots are anchored in the soil at the bottom of the pond.

Midmorning, the Sun warms the air and the lilies' flowers begin to open . . .

and open . . .

wide!

As the afternoon rolls by, more and more of the pond's wildlife enjoys the leaves and the flowers.

Slurp!

As dusk begins to settle, the lilies' leaves begin to close . . .

closing . . .

closed.

After three or four days, the water lilies' flowers drop beneath the water's surface, making room for new flower buds to bloom throughout the summer months.

A BARN OWL WAKES UP

Barn owls are expert homemakers.

Despite their name, these common owls can make themselves a cozy nest almost anywhere—in a barn, a hedgerow, a church steeple... and a tree hollow.

This female has made her nest in a tree hollow using her own pellets (undigested food), which she has shredded into a soft layer with her long claws. She will use this nest to roost in throughout the year—and often year after year! Tonight, at dusk, she wakes up hungry and ready to eat. Let's watch her get ready for the day as she heads out to hunt...

Night is coming, and this barn owl has woken up in her tree hollow.

She stretches to welcome the cool night air.

Now she's wide awake!

Strrrrrretch! Ahhhh . . . Yawn.

She settles into her day and begins to preen, which is her way of cleaning herself.

Next, she cleans her claws and toes with her beak.

Unlike most birds, barn owls do not waterproof their feathers as they preen, because they need to keep their feathers soft enough for silent flight.

Ready to face the world, she heads out to find food.

A barn owl is nearly silent when it flies, due to the structure of its soft fringe-edged feathers.

Stepping out into the night, she silently hops from the edge of her nest, and swoops into the dark.

Gliding down, down, down . . .

and—SCOOP!—she picks up a mouse in her talons.

She rests on a tree stump to eat. GULP! The owl swallows the mouse whole.

But she's only just started . . . what else will she find on her hunt tonight?

POPPIES
BLOOM IN A FIELD

Few things say summer like a field of poppies in bloom.

Blanketing a meadow with its scarlet petals, this flower—which is technically a weed—grows and blooms in direct sunlight, from late spring throughout the summer.

With a flowering season that fits neatly around a farmer's harvesting months, poppies have short life cycles, since they flower and set their seeds back into the ground before crops like grains are harvested each autumn. Used as an ingredient in medicines for hundreds of years, they are also a rich source of pollen for hungry bees. Watch as a country field begins to bloom a vibrant red...

Flower buds appear in late spring...

then bloom into bright red petals in June...

and return to a seed pod just before autumn begins.

The farmer is out checking the progress of his fields.

Poppy fields all over the world are known to stop traffic!

As spring shows its sunny face, the farmer's poppy field begins to wake up . . .
The first signs of crumpled red flowers begin to emerge, until a whole field of scarlet red fills the horizon. Spectacular!

As the end of summer approaches, the flowers begin to close, and the field returns to a sea of seed pods.
Catching a breeze, the poppies scatter their seeds in preparation for a vibrant field of poppies next summer . . .

A HORSE
GALLOPS THROUGH A MEADOW

A horse galloping freely through a meadow is as beautiful as any ballet.

Strong and majestic, horses have a natural way of moving that makes them look like elegant dancers. Horses move in two ways, both of which are called a gait.

"Natural" gaits are used to describe a horse's instinctive movements, and "ambling" gaits are techniques developed by horse trainers and riders. The gallop, which is the fastest natural gait and the method used in horse races, is a four-beat gait. In the wild, a horse will gallop when it senses danger. Let's watch a horse move freely through a country meadow . . .

For much of the morning, a chestnut horse has been walking around looking for grasses and leaves to eat.

Warming herself under the Sun, she senses something on the horizon . . .

It's a dark horse, who has found his way to the top of the hill. He wants to play!

Our chestnut horse is not sure.
She begins to trot . . .

and then canter . . .

There are four
main types of
natural horse gait:
walking, trotting,
cantering, and
galloping.

and finally she starts to gallop.

Two legs hit the ground almost together,

but one of them is a split second behind the other.

The same occurs for the front legs.

Gallop, gallop, gallop . . .
out into an open field.

Our chestnut horse is alone
again, happy to munch on grass
and go about her day without
unwanted company!

⚹ MOSS ⚹
DRINKS IN A WOODLAND RAIN SHOWER

The living, breathing heart of a forest is protected by a plant called moss.

Carpeting trees, rocks, and a forest's floor, moss helps to protect soil from the wind and rain. It feeds on water and moisture, keeping the ground fertile for other plant life around it.

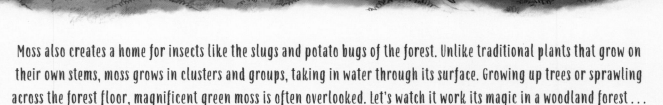

Moss also creates a home for insects like the slugs and potato bugs of the forest. Unlike traditional plants that grow on their own stems, moss grows in clusters and groups, taking in water through its surface. Growing up trees or sprawling across the forest floor, magnificent green moss is often overlooked. Let's watch it work its magic in a woodland forest . . .

The long winter months have gone and spring is here.

Hardened by the harsh winter weather, the moss has begun to dry and curl up, waiting for . . .

rain!

A light spring shower is enough to rouse the moss from its slumber.

Unfurling its short fronds to the cool air and moisture, it welcomes the droplets of water.

It drinks it in . . .

rehydrating as each drop falls.

Other animals of the forest come out to enjoy the spring shower, treading on the forest's soft carpet.

Happily fed, the moss gets back to doing what it does best: feeding the forest with moisture. A silent hero of these woods, it won't be long before it welcomes the rain once more.

A LADYBUG
TAKES TO THE AIR

The humble ladybug may look sweet, but it's also an amazing aviator.

Watching a ladybug take to the air is a bit like counting down to a space rocket launch! Powered by a pair of strong hind legs, a ladybug can fly at speeds of up to 37 miles per hour, flapping its wings 85 times a second.

Launching slowly, and with great care, the bug's bright red shell parts, or elytra, open to reveal two powerful wings that will power it into the air. The pair of hardened wing cases also act as a protective cover for its abdomen and soft body. Let's watch the world's favorite beetle take flight...

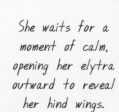

She waits for a moment of calm, opening her elytra outward to reveal her hind wings.

A little ladybug has crawled her way along a tree branch this morning, in search of sun and warmth.

She must go out to hunt and find mites to eat on a neighboring tree.

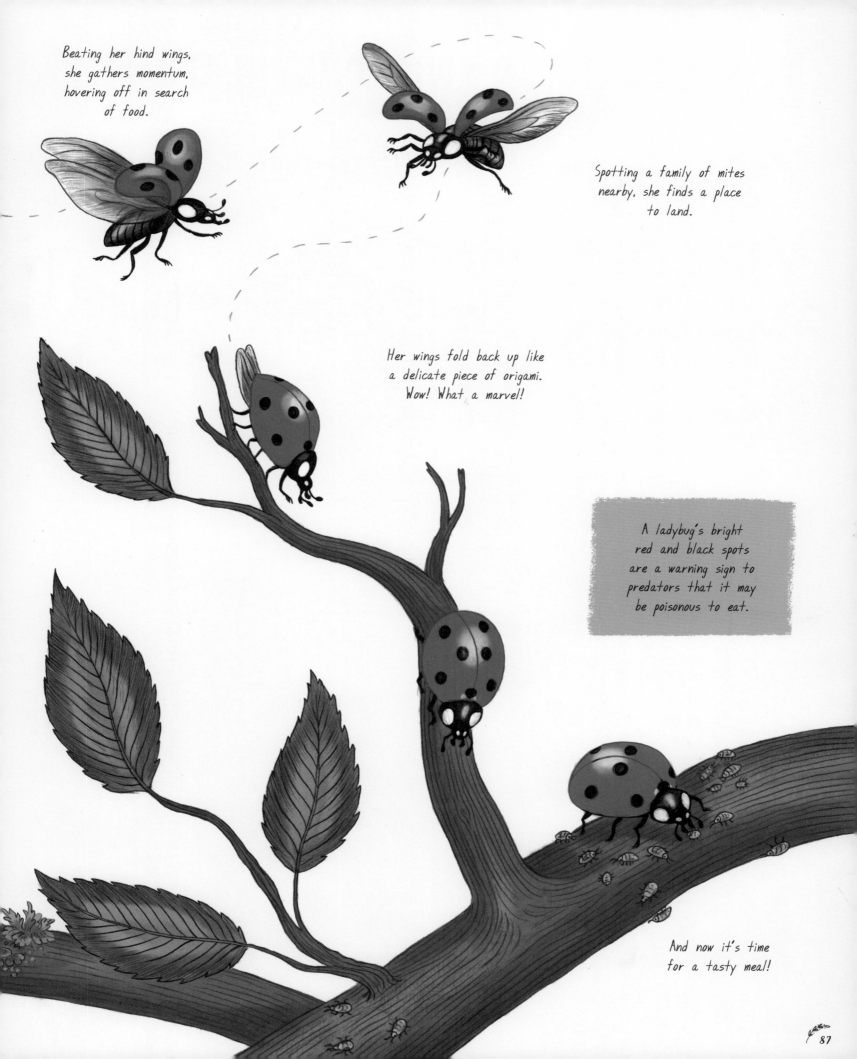

Beating her hind wings, she gathers momentum, hovering off in search of food.

Spotting a family of mites nearby, she finds a place to land.

Her wings fold back up like a delicate piece of origami. Wow! What a marvel!

A ladybug's bright red and black spots are a warning sign to predators that it may be poisonous to eat.

And now it's time for a tasty meal!

SALMON SWIM UPSTREAM

As autumn colors start to fade, one of nature's great journeys begins: the great salmon run.

When they are young, Atlantic salmon spend their time in the cool, calm waters of rivers and streams. As they grow, they swim out to sea, navigating the choppy ocean waters as adults.

After a few years, they are fully grown, and set out to return home to the rivers and streams where they were born. Here, they cross thousands of miles of water and avoid hungry predators to reach home and lay their eggs—a process known as spawning. Let's watch this journey take place over a couple of weeks...

The river levels have risen with the rain, and fully grown salmon start to make their way back to the rivers where they were born.

Scientists believe that salmon use the Earth's magnetic field to find their way back to where they were born.

Using their amazing sense of smell and built-in navigation system, salmon start their run in peak condition, able to jump over rapids and leap away from . . .

BEARS! Up and over the rapids they go, into the calm waters of the shallow river.

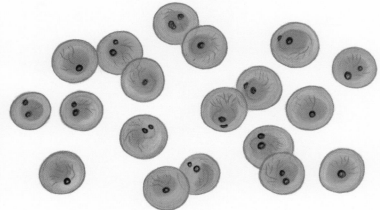

Here, the female salmon creates a nest, called a redd. It's made on the bed of the stream, among the gravel and grasses.

She lays her eggs—sometimes up to 5,000!

The female salmon buries the eggs to protect them from predators for many weeks, allowing young salmon to emerge.

When spawning is complete, many salmon will finish their life journeys here, while others make their way back out to sea.

A FLOCK OF GEESE
TAKES FLIGHT

The Canada goose is one of the largest geese in the world, and also has one of the loudest honks!

Watching this waterbird take flight with its flock is a spectacular sight of coordination and skill, as each bird gallops along a runway of water to take off into the air.

Flying in a perfect V formation, these birds migrate each year in search of food and warmer weather. When airborne, they take turns leading the way: the leader in front splits the air current, and when he tires, he moves to the back for another goose to take the lead. Let's watch them take off and make their way south for the winter . . .

"Honk, honk!" cries a restless male in this gaggle of geese.

Autumn has set in, and it's time to leave for warmer environments.

The goose gets everyone moving, raising his breast up and flapping his wings to draw their attention.

His large webbed feet race along the water's surface . . .

and he's off!

Hrink, hrink!

Honk, honk!

The rest of the flock follows closely behind, calling out in pursuit. And within moments, they are all on their way.

Forming a perfect V shape through the sky, they fly away to warmer lands.

A HARE
OUTRUNS A HUNGRY FOX

Hidden deep in a winter wonderland, mountain hares use camouflage to stay out of sight.

A bit taller than a rabbit, a mountain hare has long hind legs and large ears. During winter, its furry feet look like snowshoes.

During the summer months, hares' coats are a speckled brown color, which keeps them hidden from the many predators that roam the mountains. Come winter, the hares' coats turn a brilliant white to blend in with the snow. Their paws act a bit like snowshoes, helping them glide and hop silently across the white landscape. See one little hare in action as she races to escape a fox . . .

The hare pops his head out of his home at sunset.

A hungry fox spots the hare on her breakfast hunt . . .

He's woken up hungry and ready to go out to look for food in shrubs and plants.

Hiding in the dense woodland, the fox moves slowly . . . creeping up on the hare, who has found a tasty morsel.

She edges closer and closer, until . . .

Pounce! The fox almost catches the hare unaware.
Luckily, he is close to home . . .

The lower number of daylight hours in winter triggers the hare's brown coat to molt (shed), before it is replaced with a new white coat.

He zigzags through the snow
and in an instant . . .

he is safe. As much as she tries, the fox won't be able
to reach him here. Foiled again!

93

A KINGFISHER
DIVES UNDERWATER TO CATCH A FISH

The kingfisher lives up to its name.

With a brightly colored coat, its sharp beak is aerodynamically shaped for fishing, allowing it to dive at lightning speed with minimum splash.

These birds will happily hunt fish larger and heavier than themselves, though small fish like minnows make up some of their favorite meals. Kingfishers build their nests by burrowing into the sandy soil of a stream bank and use the branches and logs along a waterway as lookout perches for food. They catch several fish each day, while raising their families and defending their nests. Watch one dive into a stream filled with fish in the blink of an eye...

Perched on a log, this kingfisher has spotted his chosen fish and begins to bob his head.

Taking off, he flies above the stream, beating his wings silently while his head now stays completely still.

The design of the kingfisher's beak is so clever that many Japanese bullet train designs mimic its shape.

He dives vertically, headfirst, with his eyelids closed and beak slightly open . . .

Splash!

The dive sends shock waves through the water.

Before the minnow can even react, this kingfisher has caught his meal . . .

and carried it back to his perch to gobble up. Soon it will be time to dive again . . .

A HARVEST MOUSE
SEARCHES FOR SUPPER

A harvest mouse is an expert, agile climber.

With a strong tail that acts a bit like a fifth leg, it can climb up the stems of wheatgrass, crops, or flowers in seconds.

Once at the top, it finds seeds with its front paws and removes their husks with its teeth. Mainly an herbivore, this mouse harvests throughout the year! In the spring, it eats grasses, buds on bushes, and nectar from flowers. Come summer, it will feed on the seeds, or kernels, of crops like wheat, as well as small insects, such as caterpillars. Come autumn, the mouse will work its way through a berry bush. Let's watch one catch its summer feast . . .

Summer is here, and this little harvest mouse is on her daily journey to find food.

Wrapping her tail around a stem, she climbs up . . . and up, until she reaches the top of the length of wheatgrass.

The tail of a British harvest mouse is called a prehensile tail, which has adapted to hold and grasp onto objects—just like another paw.

Here, she sways in the summer breeze, surveying the field.

Back . . . and forth . . . back . . . and forth.

Breaking off a kernel of wheat with her teeth, she holds it in her front paws . . .

removing the husk and gnawing through it. Delicious!

Up here, she is in danger of being spotted by an owl . . . time to scurry down!

Using her tail as a clamp, she climbs her way down, back to the safety of the thick grass. On to find more food!

AN OYSTER
MAKES A PEARL

The hard shell of an oyster hides a precious gemstone: a luminous pearl.

This gemstone begins its life when an oyster senses an intruder, such as a small parasite, entering its shell.

The inner part of the oyster's shell is lined with something called nacre, which is also known as mother-of-pearl. In order to protect itself from the intruder, the oyster covers it with nacre, adding layer upon layer to slowly encase it. Over many years, the pearl forms, growing smooth and round with each year. Let's watch one form in the cool ocean waters . . .

The oyster's hard shell opens and closes gently.

Feeding on algae, she has a strong sense of something that may be a friend— or foe.

Snap!

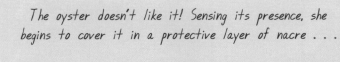

False alarm!

But just as she opens up again, something unwanted makes its way inside . . .

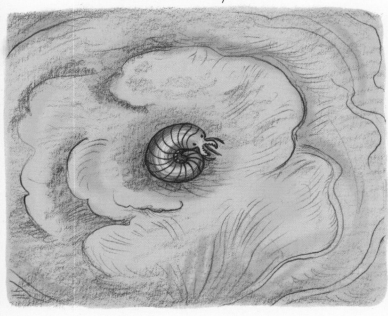

The oyster doesn't like it! Sensing its presence, she begins to cover it in a protective layer of nacre . . .

Layer . . . after layer . . .

After many years, a small, smooth pearl is formed.

Oysters are from a family of sea creatures called mollusks. Any mollusk that produces a shell can also produce a pearl—such as a clam or a mussel.

What an amazing thing to make from an uninvited guest!

✤ A WOLF ✤
HOWLS TO HIS PACK

Nighttime has fallen, but the wolves of this forest are just waking up.

Known for their spine-tingling howls, wolves use their voices to communicate.

A howl may mean a number of things: a call to ask a wolf pack to meet up, a signal to let the pack know a wolf's location;, or a warning for others to stay away.

Contrary to popular belief, a wolf howls on any given night–not just when the Moon is full!
So before you go to bed tonight, watch as a wolf calls out to his pack...

Dusk has turned to night and a young grey wolf has woken up slightly later than his pack.

Barely visible on this misty evening, the Moon still illuminates the forest floor.

Ahoooo!

He makes a call out to
his pack. Lifting his head high,
he howls.

The sound travels far and wide across the
valley below.

Ahoooo!

Known to roam long
distances, his pack
hears his call and
signals back.

"Ahoooo!" calls the pack's mother in return. "Ahoooo!"

Her other wolf cubs join in. "Ahoooo!"
comes the chorus.

Picking up their call, the young
wolf heads off in their direction.

Using his strong sense of smell, he soon locates his pack, and
together, They head into the dark night to find food . . .

SLOW DOWN TODAY

Now that you've witnessed the many workings of nature, it's time to experience them for yourself. This morning, take some time to go outside and connect yourself to the great outdoors . . . and then watch how it changes the way you see and hear the things around you.

You can do this exercise sitting up or lying down.

Take a couple of big, deep breaths.

Close your eyes if you'd like to.

Begin to wiggle your fingers and your toes.

Move your head from side to side.

What can you hear?

The leaves rustling . . .

a frog croaking in a stream nearby.

a bird singing . . .

What can you feel?

The Sun on your face . . .

the wind in your hair . . .

warm grass, all around you.

Take another deep breath in, and stretch
your arms up to welcome the morning.

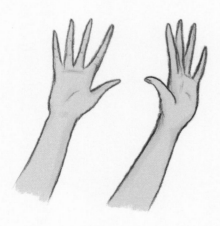

A new day has arrived.

FURTHER READING

Find out more about nature and mindfulness with the help of an adult.

NATURE

American Horticulture Society

AHSGARDENING.ORG

The American Horticultural Society is a national gardening organization made up of gardeners, horticultural professionals, and partner organizations from all across North America.

The Honeybee Conservancy

THEHONEYBEECONSERVANCY.ORG

The Honeybee Conservancy is a nonprofit organization that works to educate communities, support research, promote outreach, and build bee habitats.

Marine Conservation Institute

MARINE-CONSERVATION.ORG

Marine Conservation Institute works to protect the ocean and its marine ecosystems so that they will be around for years to come.

National Audubon Society

AUDUBON.ORG

The National Audubon Society protects birds and their habitats across the Americas. They implement on-the-ground conservation efforts, use science and advocacy, and educate communities to do this.

National Parks Conservation Association

NPCA.ORG

The National Park Conservation Association (NPCA) works to protect and enhance the National Parks System across the United States.

National Wildlife Federation

NWF.ORG

The National Wildlife Federation works to protect America's wildlife and unite Americans in this cause.

The Nature Conservancy

NATURE.ORG

The Nature Conservancy is a nonprofit environmental organization that works to battle climate change, protect nature, provide food sustainability, and build healthier cities.

Sierra Club Foundation

SIERRACLUB.ORG

The Sierra Club works to educate communities and encourage people to explore, enjoy, and protect the Earth.

Wildlife Conservation Society

WCS.ORG

The Wildlife Conservation Society (WCS) works to conserve the natural world and protect its wildlife.

MINDFULNESS

Child Mind Institute

CHILDMIND.ORG

The Child Mind Institute is a national nonprofit dedicated to supporting children and families struggling with mental health.

Mindful Littles

MINDFULLITTLES.ORG

Mindful Littles is a nonprofit organization that offers well-being practices and service learning for elementary school children, parents, caregivers, and educators.

Mindfulness 4 Youth

MINDFULNESS4YOUTH.ORG

Mindfulness 4 Youth is a nonprofit children's charity that works to provide access to mindfulness and movement instruction to schools and underserved areas.

SELECTED BIBLIOGRAPHY

ATLANTIC SALMON TRUST, "KNOWLEDGE ZONE":
WWW.ATLANTICSALMONTRUST.ORG/KNOWLEDGE-ZONE

BRITISH DRAGONFLY SOCIETY, "DRAGONFLIES":
WWW.BRITISH-DRAGONFLIES.ORG.UK/ODONATA/DRAGONFLIES-2

BUTTERFLY SCHOOL, A SERVICE OF THE EDUCATION
DEPARTMENT OF THE SOPHIA M. SACHS BUTTERFLY HOUSE &
EDUCATION CENTER IN ST. LOUIS, MISSOURI:
WWW.BUTTERFLYSCHOOL.ORG

CANAL AND RIVER TRUST, "A SPOTTER'S GUIDE TO
WATERWAY WILDLIFE":
WWW.CANALRIVERTRUST.ORG.UK/ENJOY-THE-WATERWAYS/CANAL
-AND-RIVER-WILDLIFE/A-SPOTTERS-GUIDE-TO-WATERWAY-WILDLIFE

DK FIND OUT!, "WEATHER":
WWW.DKFINDOUT.COM/UK/EARTH/WEATHER

FELL, ANDY. "HOW SUNFLOWERS MOVE TO FOLLOW THE SUN."
BERKELEY UNIVERSITY,. AUGUST, 4 2016. SEE:
WWW.NATURE.BERKELEY.EDU/NEWS/2016/08/SUNFLOWERS-MOVE-CLOCK

KEW ROYAL BOTANIC GARDENS, "A TALE OF TWO POPPIES":
WWW.KEW.ORG/READ-AND-WATCH/TALE-TWO-POPPIES

MARINE BIOLOGICAL ASSOCIATION, "FACT SHEET: STARFISH":
WWW.MBA.AC.UK/FACT-SHEET-STARFISH

MY HORSE UNIVERSITY, "NATURAL AND ARTIFICIAL GAITS OF
THE HORSE":
WWW.MYHORSEUNIVERSITY.COM/SINGLE-POST/2017/09/25
/NATURAL-AND-ARTIFICIAL-GAITS-OF-THE-HORSE

NATIONAL GEOGRAPHIC, "ANIMALS: INVERTEBRATES
PICTURES & FACTS":
WWW.NATIONALGEOGRAPHIC.COM/ANIMALS/INVERTEBRATES

NATIONAL GEOGRAPHIC KIDS, "DISCOVER: ANIMALS":
WWW.NATGEOKIDS.COM/UK/CATEGORY/DISCOVER/ANIMALS

NATIONAL OCEAN SERVICE, "WHY DOES THE OCEAN
HAVE WAVES?":
WWW.OCEANSERVICE.NOAA.GOV/FACTS/WAVESINOCEAN.HTML

NATURAL HISTORY MUSEUM, "HOW DO OYSTERS
MAKE PEARLS?":
WWW.NHM.AC.UK/DISCOVER/QUICK-QUESTIONS/HOW-DO-OYSTERS
-MAKE-PEARLS.HTML

RSPB, WILDLIFE GUIDES: "BIRD A-Z":
WWW.RSPB.ORG.UK/BIRDS-AND-WILDLIFE/WILDLIFE-GUIDES/BIRD-A-Z

RSPB, WILDLIFE GUIDES: "INSECTS AND OTHER
INVERTEBRATES":
WWW.RSPB.ORG.UK/BIRDS-AND-WILDLIFE/WILDLIFE-GUIDES/
OTHER-GARDEN-WILDLIFE/INSECTS-AND-OTHER-INVERTEBRATES

SCOTTISH WILDLIFE TRUST, "SPECIES FINDER":
WWW.SCOTTISHWILDLIFETRUST.ORG.UK/SPECIES/MOUNTAIN-HARE

THE BARN OWL TRUST:
WWW.BARNOWLTRUST.ORG.UK

THE BRITISH BEEKEEPERS ASSOCIATION, "BEE FACTS":
WWW.BBKA.ORG.UK/PAGES/FAQS/CATEGORY/BEE-FACTS

THE MALARIA ATLAS PROJECT, "MOSQUITO MALARIAL
VECTORS" :
WWW.MAP.OX.AC.UK/MOSQUITO-MALARIA-VECTORS

THE MAMMAL SOCIETY, "FULL SPECIES HUB":
WWW.MAMMAL.ORG.UK/SPECIES-HUB/FULL-SPECIES-HUB/DISCOVER-MAMMALS

THE ROYAL HORTICULTURAL SOCIETY, "NYMPHAEA ALBA":
WWW.RHS.ORG.UK/PLANTS/11623/NYMPHAEA-ALBA-(H)/DETAILS

THE WILDLIFE TRUSTS, "MAMMALS":
WWW.WILDLIFETRUSTS.ORG/WILDLIFE-EXPLORER/MAMMALS

THE WILDLIFE TRUSTS, "WILDFLOWERS":
WWW.WILDLIFETRUSTS.ORG/WILDLIFE-EXPLORER/WILDFLOWERS

YOUNG PEOPLE'S TRUST FOR THE ENVIRONMENT,
"FACTSHEETS":
WWW.YPTE.ORG.UK/FACTSHEETS/BROWSE

INDEX

A

ANT 64–65
ATLANTIC SALMON 88–89
AUTUMN 16–17, 50–51, 54–55, 80–81

B

BARN OWL 78–79
BAT 18–19
BEACH 32–33
BEE 2–3, 28–29, 41
BIRD 8–9, 12–13, 26–27, 56–57, 60–61, 70–71, 90–91, 94–95
BLACKBIRD 12–13
BLUEBELL 36–37
BUTTERFLY 6–7

C

CANADA GOOSE 90–91
CAT 42–43
CATERPILLAR 6
CHERRY BLOSSOM 62–63
CHICK 26–27, 60–61
CHICKEN 60–61
CHRYSALIS 6–7
CLOUD 14–15, 58–59
CONDENSATION 4–5, 58–59

D

DAWN CHORUS 12–13
DEW 4–5
DRAGONFLY 74–75
DUCK 8–9
DUCKLING 8–9

E

ECDYSIS 46–47
ECHOLOCATION 18–19
EGG 26–27, 34–35, 60–61, 89

F

FERN 66–67
FERTILIZATION 2–3, 34, 89
FIDDLEHEAD 66–67
FISH 88–89
FLIGHT 7, 18–19, 68–69, 74–75, 78–79, 86–87, 90–91, 94–95
FLOWER 2–3, 28, 36–37, 40–41, 62–63, 76–77, 80–81
FLY AGARIC 49
FOREST 36–37, 48–49, 66–67, 70–71, 84–85
FOX 22–23, 92–93
FROG 34–35
FROGSPAWN 34
FUNGUS 48–49

G

GASTROPOD	52–53
GOOSE	90–91
GREY SQUIRREL	16–17
GREY WOLF	100–101

H

HARE	92–93
HARVEST MOUSE	96–97
HELIOTROPISM	40–41
HEN	60–61
HIBERNATION	16–17
HIVE	28–29
HONEYBEE	28–29
HORSE	82–83
HUNTING	10–11, 18–19, 38–39, 42–43, 70–71, 72–73, 74–75, 78–79, 92–93, 94–95

I

ICE CRYSTAL	24–25
INSECT	2–3, 6–7, 10–11, 28–29, 64–65, 68–69, 74–75, 86–87

K

KINGFISHER	94–95

L

LADYBUG	86–87
LARVA	65
LEAF	4–5, 54–55, 64–65, 66–67
LIGHTNING	14–15
LONG-EARED BAT	18–19
LUNAR CYCLE	30–31

M

MALLARD	8-9
MEADOW	82-83
METAMORPHOSIS	6-7, 34-35
METEOR	44-45
MIGRATION	88-89, 90-91
MOLE	38-39
MOLTING	46-47, 92-93
MOON	30-31
MOSQUITO	68-69, 74-75
MOSS	84-85
MOUNTAIN HARE	92-93
MOUSE	42-43, 96-97
MUSHROOM	48-49
MYCELIUM	48-49

N

NESTING	26-27, 64-65, 78, 89, 94
NIGHTTIME	18-19, 22-23, 30-31, 44-45, 78-79, 100-101

O

OCEAN	32-33, 72-73, 88-89, 98-99
ORB WEAVER	10-11
OWL	78-79
OYSTER	98-99

P

PEARL	98-99
PHOTOSYNTHESIS	54-55
POLLINATION	2-3
POND LIFE	8-9, 34-35, 74-75, 76-77, 88-89, 94-95
POPPY	80-81
PUPA	6-7

R

RAIN	14-15, 84-85
RAINBOW	20-21
ROBIN	12-13

S

SALMON	88-89
SEA LIFE	72-73, 88-89, 98-99
SEA STAR	72-73
SHOOTING STAR	44-45
SNAIL	52-53
SNAKE	46-47
SNOWFLAKE	24-25
SPACE	44-45
SPARROW	12-13, 56-57
SPAWNING	88-89
SPIDER	10-11
SPRING	2-3, 40-41, 62-63, 66-67, 81, 84-85
SQUIRREL	16-17
STAMEN	2-3
STARFISH	72-73
STIGMA	2-3
SUMMER	14-15, 28-29, 52-53, 74-75, 76-77, 80-81, 96-97
SUNFLOWER	40-41
SUNSET	50-51

T

TADPOLE   34-35
THUNDERSTORM   14-15
TREE   54-55, 62-63, 70-71

U

UNDERGROUND   36, 38-39, 48-49

W

WARBLER   12-13
WATER LILY   76-77
WATER VOLE   76-77
WAVE   32-33
WEATHER   14-15, 20-21, 24-25, 58-59
WEAVER ANT   64-65
WEB   10-11
WINTER   17, 24-25, 92-93
WOLF   100-101
WOOD BLEWIT   48-49
WOODPECKER   70-71

Library of Congress Control Number 2019955023
ISBN 978-1-4197-4838-7

The illustrations were created in pen and ink and colored digitally.
Set in Organika, Above the Sky, and Blunt.

Text copyright © 2020 Rachel Williams
Illustrations copyright © 2020 Freya Hartas
Designed by Nicola Price
Edited by Eryl Nash and Jenny Broom

Printed and bound in China
10 9 8 7 6 5 4 3

Abrams Books are available at special discounts when purchased in quantity for premiums and
promotions as well as fundraising or educational use. Special editions can also be created to
specification. For details, contact specialsales@abramsbooks.com or the address below.

MIX
Paper from
responsible sources
FSC® C104723

ABRAMS The Art of Books
195 Broadway, New York, NY 10007
abramsbooks.com

For my Mum, Barbara.
Giver of gifts and grower of green things. –R.W.

For Mum, who has the most beautiful garden, which is home
to many of the creatures in this book. –F.H.